*France
under
Napoleon*

FRANCE
UNDER NAPOLEON

by Louis Bergeron

TRANSLATED BY
R. R. PALMER

Princeton University Press
Princeton, New Jersey

Copyright © 1981 by Princeton University Press

Published by Princeton University Press, Princeton, New Jersey
In the United Kingdom: Princeton University Press, Guildford, Surrey

Translated from Louis Bergeron, *L'Episode napoléonien. Aspects
intérieurs, 1799-1815*. Paris, © Editions du Seuil, 1972

Library of Congress Cataloging in Publication Data will be found on the last printed
page of this book

Clothbound editions of Princeton University Press books are printed on acid-free
paper, and binding materials are chosen for strength and durability

Printed in the United States of America by Princeton
University Press, Princeton, New Jersey

CONTENTS

PART TWO
France from 1800 to 1815

TRANSLATOR'S PREFACE

This is a unique book in that it is about France under Napoleon, and not about Napoleon himself, nor his conquests, his empire, or his impact on Europe. The personal importance of Napoleon Bonaparte is by no means minimized, but the theme is the condition of France and the French people in the years immediately following their great Revolution. Much has been written on the causes of the French Revolution, and on the course of the Revolution itself; here we have an analysis of its outcome, which was perhaps more significant and more lasting. Much has also been heard in this country about the new social history of which the French have been eminent practitioners for the past thirty years. Most work of this kind has been devoted to the centuries preceding the Revolution, or to the nineteenth century with its problems of urbanization and industrialism. The interval between them is treated here by Louis Bergeron for the first time at book length in the same spirit. Readers versed in the social history of the Old Régime may see here how it turned out. Those concerned with the social history of the nineteenth century may find a firm point of departure. An incidental result is to illuminate the question, debated since Alexis de Tocqueville, of whether the Revolution marked an abrupt break, or an underlying continuity, in French life and institutions.

The original title of the book, published in 1972, was *L'Episode napoléonien: aspects intérieurs, 1799-1815.* The word "episode" reflects the fact that the book was one of a series on the history of France since the Revolution, and the subtitle, "internal aspects," is a reminder that another volume in the same series (much less innovative) dealt with French foreign policy and expansion at the time. But to call these really epochal years an "episode" also reveals an historiographical attitude. An "episode" suggests transiency. It is a peculiarity of the new social history to give slight attention to passing events, and to concentrate rather on more permanent "structures" and on developments that can occur only over long periods of time. The mode is analytic, not narrative. It is another peculiarity to say little about individual persons or their influence. The influence of Bonaparte pervades the book, but we see him as an actual human being only tangentially. As for other persons, over four hundred are actually named, but the reader is hardly expected to remember them, for most of them figure only as examples of social or occupational categories. The examples may be vivid, but it is the groups that matter. The book reflects an interest in what has been somewhat awkwardly called prosopography, the study of persons having a common role, such as Napoleon's marshals, in terms of their social background, family connections, marriages, property, income, previous occupation or political record during the Revolution.

Signs of the new social history are evident not only in the careful class analysis, particularly of the bourgeoisie and both the old and the newly emerging elites, but also in the incorporation of bits of detailed local history into the national picture, in the use of historical demography to explain changes in population and in the family, and in the concern with quantitative data, shown not in formulas or graphs but in a taste for percentages, the construction of maps, and a curiosity about personal incomes. Among social historians, the author is more than usually strong in economics and economic history, as is evident in his treatment of fiscal and financial developments, the functions of property and capital, and the tensions between the stubborn persistence of older forms and the beginnings of industrialization. While he doubts that such dating is necessary or useful, he holds that if a specific date had to be named for the Industrial Revolution in France it would fall within these years under Napoleon.

It has often been found, as a shortcoming of social history, that it underestimates the political element in human affairs, and that it tends to reduce the history of ideas to a description of "collective mentalities." Some of the most interesting pages in this book, however, deal with the survival of political life under the Bonapartist regime, at least in its early years. Here the author touches on intellectual history also, in his discussion of Mme de Staël and Benjamin Constant. Religion, science, the general movement of ideas, and the reaction against the Enlightenment form the substance of the concluding chapter. We thus have, on a compact and manageable scale, a specimen of that "total history" at which authors of more weighty volumes have aimed.

History in France has been characteristically seen more as a science than in the English-speaking countries. Our author's tone is that of a scientific worker, active in the pursuit of new knowledge, examining hitherto unknown sources, conscious of being one of many operating on a new frontier, and often referring to the findings of his contemporaries. The book in its original is replete with footnotes citing the contributions of others, and contains a substantial bibliography, mostly consisting of highly specialized recent monographs and articles in relatively inaccessible journals, virtually all in French. Since a translation is designed for those who do not read the original language easily, and since those who can benefit from such apparatus may consult the original, I have omitted the bibliography and kept only a fraction of the notes, mainly those in acknowledgment of direct quotations, a few in which archival sources are cited, and a few referring to works in English, a language with which Bergeron is well acquainted. I have also added a few references to works published since the French edition of 1972. The notes that remain may constitute a representative bibliography in themselves.

Louis Bergeron is a graduate of the Ecole Normale Supérieure and since 1971 has been a director of studies at the Ecole des hautes études en science sociales in Paris. He has been a visiting professor at Cornell University. His publications have ranged from the general to the extremely specific. He is the author of a two-volume work, abundantly illustrated and designed for general readers, published in 1968, and entitled (in French) "The European Revolutions and the Division of the World, 1715-1914." This was soon followed by a book translated into German, "The Age of the European Revolution, 1780-1848." He then became active in planning, supervising and contributing to various more specialized and collective undertakings. For a series on world economic and social history he edited the volume on the period 1730-1840, for which he wrote the chapter on the Industrial Revolution in England. With collaborators, he has brought out a number of computerized and multibiographical studies of the personnel of the First Empire. He has published articles in the *Annales: Sociétés, Economies, Civilisations,* without claiming membership in the "*Annales* school" or any other. His principal work is his *thèse de doctorat*, published after years of preparation, on "Bankers, merchants and manufacturers in Paris from the Directory to the Empire." The French titles and other particulars relating to these works are given below in the appendix. For the future, he plans further studies of the social structure of French financial, commercial and industrial capitalism in the nineteenth century.

The present small book is thus a condensation of very wide knowledge and research. Bergeron has no responsibility for the translation, which he has not seen, but he has taken the occasion to rewrite or modify a few passages in the original. I am indebted to him for his assistance on a few thorny problems, and for his cordial cooperation throughout. I should like also to express my thanks to the National Humanities Center in North Carolina, where during an all too brief fellowship much of this translation was done.

R. R. Palmer

FOREWORD

In brief, what meaning is there in the order in which these fifteen years of the internal history of France are presented?

Part One of the book is devoted to the domestic program of Napoleon Bonaparte. It could hardly be otherwise. The most important development of these years—and especially of the first eight or nine years of the new century—was in fact the intense activity of the new Chief of State. It was his political genius, as it is generally agreed to call it, to combine his own clear and strongly held personal ideas and convictions, reinforced by his great individual prestige, with a sure sense of the necessary and the possible in revolutionary France—after ten years of revolution. "My policy is to govern men as the great number wish to be governed. That, I think, is the way to recognize the sovereignty of the people." While implacably suppressing the most actively opposed minorities, he overcame the apathy and the wait-and-see attitude of the majority of the French. In matters of social hierarchy and the administrative system he forced upon the French, who from citizens were soon to become subjects again, a coherent construction which he intended to be permanent, and which reflected his taste for uniformity, symmetry and efficiency, the signs of a rational organization in which a single mind transmitted impulses to the most distant members. What we see as rigid or even oppressive in the survivals of the Napoleonic system were at the time the source of its strength, making of it a model to be envied, and one of unequaled modernity.

Part Two, while not claiming to set up an opposition between France and the First Consul and Emperor, who by no means lacked popular support, is nevertheless addressed to everything that eluded his grasp. The importance of the period and of the man are unavoidably reduced when seen in the light of long gradual movements, deep tendencies, or elements of resistance. The period in this way may seem only an episode. The régime never had time to consolidate its base; perhaps it never had more than the appearance of stability. The demographic behavior of the French people escaped it; pop-

ulation growth slackened although Napoleon would have wished
a high fecundity to strengthen his empire. It was only with reservations that the social body adapted itself to the Napoleonic structure; the fusion of elites was only imperfectly realized. One of the
pillars of the State, the Catholic clergy, defected, undermined by
the progress of ultramontanism. In the deeper life of the nation it
was economic activity that showed the most independence, or the
least capacity for adaptation to a régime whose ideal was for everything to be perfectly controlled. The agricultural and rural world
evolved at its own rhythms, which had little to do with the political
universe. Deeply marked by the Revolution, it was hardly affected
by the Empire. Industrial production and commercial exchanges
reacted immediately to the shifts in international politics, but the
renovation of industrial structures depended on a combination of
conditions that was modified only slowly. Let us not deceive our-
selves—France changed very little from 1800 to 1815. Paradoxically, Napoleon was both behind and ahead of his time, the last of
the enlightened despots, and a prophet of the modern State.

PART ONE

*The Napoleonic Blueprint
for the State
and Society*

I

The Régime

As for 18 Brumaire and the Constitution of the Year VIII (1799), we need not hesitate to assign a special importance (although such will not be our practice) to the political event itself, and to the juridical text. Contemporaries were inevitably uninformed, and even today we do not know, from documents, all the elements in the Brumaire conspiracy. As important a point as the psychology and intentions of Bonaparte himself at the moment remains a matter for further exploration.

Yet the coup d'état of General Bonaparte was not like those that preceded it. We could, if we liked, classify it among events that seem greater in retrospect. It may be argued that there was no sudden new departure. The words "French Republic" remained in official use even after the hereditary Empire was proclaimed. And it is both easy and instructive to note the important ways in which the First Consul simply followed the methods and policies of the Directors whom he had nevertheless overthrown. From Thermidor of the Year II (1794) until 1804 it is also true that the same society of beneficiaries of the Revolution, by successive readjustments, worked out the detailed conditions of its political survival and assurance of its social domination.

And yet! We who have been witnesses to the evolution and political behavior of capitalist countries in the twentieth century are inevitably aware of the phenomena of the personalization of power and the crisis of parliamentary institutions. We are therefore tempted to reread more attentively the history of parliamentary assemblies and of their asphyxiation that may follow only a few years after their omnipotence, hence also to reconsider the history of this "soldier, son of the Revolution," as Bonaparte called himself, who by one forcible stroke became a sovereign of a special kind, a monarch in fact before being so in law. Important as the change of régime was (and its full meaning became apparent only as it began to function), even more so was the meaning that Bonaparte himself attributed to his own political advent. His rule was to mark the close of the Revolution, a return to order and stability, a rejoining of the history of France with the first stage of the Revolution, but only the first stage.

There is thus no doubt about the interpretation to be given to the historic role of Napoleon Bonaparte. For the rest of the world, indeed, he remained the fearsome propagator of the Revolution, or the admirable instrument of reason governing the world, of progress of the spirit in its long "discourse with time" (Hegel). But for France? With Brumaire came the time for filtering or decanting what had happened. Bonaparte belongs to the Revolution, surely, in matters that seemed irreversible at the time—civil equality, the destruction of feudalism, the ruin of the privileged position of the Catholic Church. As for the rest, the enjoyment of liberties, the form of political institutions, there had been since 1789 so much instability, so many contradictions between grand principles and the practice of governments, so much persistent uncertainty on the outcome of the war and the unity of the nation, that the field lay open for a strong man who, on condition of preserving the essential conquests of the Revolution, would do something new in the matter of government and refuse to be embarrassed by scruples. By anchoring France securely to the shores that the Constituent Assembly had been unwilling to leave, Bonaparte accomplished somewhat late in the day that "revolution from above" of which the old monarchy had been incapable. The political trade-off was a certain number of amputations of the immediate Revolutionary inheritance, a few backward movements, and disconcerting borrowings from the Old Régime. In a sense, the dynamism of Bonaparte and his rigorous administration revived the experiment of enlightened despotism, somewhat belatedly, since in the setting of Western Europe it was already a bit out of date.

1. POLITICAL INSTITUTIONS:
STRUCTURE AND EVOLUTION

Sovereignty of the People, Representative System:
Fictions and Realities

When Bonaparte was officially received by the Directory at the Luxembourg Palace on 10 December 1797, he spoke of the need of "founding the happiness of the French people on better organic laws." By this he doubtless only expressed sentiments shared by many of the "republicans of order," for whom the double danger from counterrevolution and democracy required a strengthening of the State, considered as the depository of the Revolution. But until 18 Brumaire he had not set forth his views on this matter more explicitly. The first indications appeared in the procedure for preparation of the new constitution destined to replace the one of the Year III. The task was confided on 19 Brumaire to the provisional consuls and to two legislative committees, drawn from the former Five Hundred and *Anciens,** but the work dragged on too slowly for Bonaparte's taste, and after 11 Frimaire VIII (2 December 1799) it was carried on in his own house and under his direction. He was thus able, by forcing the hand of the constitution makers on the matter of executive power, to get himself designated to the supreme magistracy without any prior election. The constitution was then put into effect without waiting for the referendum or plebiscite to which it had to be submitted. Thus a kind of second coup d'état was effected, by which Bonaparte confiscated for himself the constituent power that had been one of the first conquests of the Estates General of 1789.

Such an attitude reflected an essential conception of Bonaparte's: the idea of a transfer of sovereignty, which in law emanated from the people, to a chief of government enjoying the public confidence, and by way of reciprocity dedicating himself entirely to the general

---

* The Five Hundred and Anciens were the two houses of the Legislative Body under the Directory, the Anciens of course being simply the elder or senior house. The reader may wish to clarify the sequence of events by consulting the Chronological Outline in the Appendix. (Trans.)

good. It was not a revolutionary idea, though under exceptional circumstances the dictatorship of the Committee of Public Safety had been inspired by it in practice. But to call it "reactionary" would be to forget that it could be derived from a Rousseauist theory of the social contract, and that it corresponded to the thinking of more than one *philosophe*—Diderot in particular.

Men being made to be governed, what remained of those other revolutionary conquests—the right to have and to elect representatives? As for the suffrage, Napoleon again made it universal; if he could allow it, it was because he disarmed it by narrowly limiting its functions. The new thing was the recourse to the plebiscite; but to reply by "yes" or "no," or by abstention, was less a political choice than an expression of feeling, of overall confidence granted or refused to a man. Exercised in local or "primary" assemblies, the vote did not have the purpose of designating public representatives or officials, but served only as the base of a system of electoral colleges, which became true "intermediate bodies" between the government and the governed. In any case, universal suffrage had few occasions to operate. Napoleon held no more plebiscites after 1804. The electoral colleges set up by the Constitution of the Year X (1802) were formed for life, and received no new members until the vacancies became a third of their number; there would be in fact only a single renewal.

Legislative assemblies did not disappear with the Constitution of the Year VIII, but this was only because Bonaparte had to make concessions to the Brumairians, and notably to Sieyès, that is to a group that remained as firmly attached to a representative system as to reinforcement of the executive. Bonaparte himself was resolutely hostile to assemblies and he was determined, if he had to preserve the appearance, to confine them to purely formal concerns. As early as 1797, writing to Talleyrand, he described the ideal legislative power as "having no rank in the Republic, impassive, having neither eyes nor ears for what surrounds it. . . . We would no longer be inundated with a thousand capricious laws that cancel each other by their own absurdity, so that we are constituted as a nation by three hundred in-folio lawbooks." The regression was considerable—but it had begun under the Directors—from the early

Revolutionary assemblies, respected organs of legislation and even of government, to the Tribunate and the Legislative Body of the Year VIII, of which the former debated and the latter voted on bills which originated outside their own chambers, all within time limits set by the government. But although their members were at first simply appointed, and then chosen from prescribed lists of candidates, these two councils, which also were quite small, were not purely passive or inclined to the opinions expected of them by the executive. The Tribunate, more brilliant in composition and more courageous in its personalities, suffered the consequences by being purged, and later abolished. The Legislative Body, more mediocre, more docile, and more controlled in its recruitment, survived.

The assembly nearest the heart of Napoleon Bonaparte was the Senate. In a society which was in process of organizing itself on the double criterion of wealth and service to the State, from the "notable" who became an elector to the "grand dignitary" who was a noble of the Empire, the senator before being finally installed found himself granted the considerable salary of 25,000 francs a year, without prejudice to further emoluments. The presidency of the Senate was at first a consolation prize for Sieyès. There were at first only 60 members—31 named directly by the First Consul, and 29 co-opted by them; but by 1813 there were 141 members, since in the Year XII (1804) princes and grand dignitaries were added as of right, and later many others were named by the Emperor, including some for the benefit of regions recently annexed. The method of recruitment and the considerable advantages of membership made the Senate an amenable and even servile body. The timidity of its efforts to limit the disturbing growth of Bonaparte's powers in the Year X, and then again in the Year XII, was matched by its cowardice in 1814, when its courage returned only after the master was defeated in war. "The adapter rather than preserver of the Constitution," as Charles Durand has said, it exercised in fact a legislative power that responded to the unofficial and indirect solicitations of its master. The *senatas-consulte* was used from the beginning on the occasion of important political actions—the condemnation of 130 Jacobins to deportation in 1801; the amnesty of the émigrés in 1802—and to give a basis in law for the progressive drift of the Consulate into the Empire. After 1804 the Senate no longer even had the competition of the plebiscite, and its character of providing "legislation above the laws" was reinforced.

Public Liberties

Let us set aside temporarily these constitutional arrangements. The decay of representative institutions was only a part, in fact, of a general encroachment on public liberties, and in particular on freedom of expression. In both cases Bonaparte argued from circumstances. The very principle of the coup d'état was to put an end to what he called "anarchy"—that is, the dangers of a royalist counterrevolution and of a renewal of Jacobinism or Babouvism. Stabilization could come only with an authoritarian Republic. Conciliation, or appeasement, was clearly one side of the consular and imperial policy. But the other side was rigorous control, or repression. Silence was to be imposed on the factions and troublemakers of both sides. Hence no opportunity should be left for the expression of political differences, either in parliamentary debate or through the medium of the press. Although the Constitution of the Year VIII, without any solemn declaration, briefly enumerated the rights of equality, liberty, security (of person) and property, it was only the last that received an effective guarantee, both in the Civil Code and the Concordat. The partial infringement on equality will be considered later.

As for liberty, there is no doubt that Bonaparte considered freedom of the press a public scourge. The press existed in his eyes only for service to the State and as an instrument of propaganda. From his first campaign in Italy to the height of the Empire this conception was realized in three stages. Even before the Consulate Bonaparte had used short-lived journals, directly inspired by him, for his own purposes, and this was later his method when he composed anonymous articles to be inserted in the *Moniteur*, replying to an opposition which at the beginning of the Consulate still kept some means of open expression. Thereafter he counted on his ministers of the interior to fulfill the same function of guidance for the journals that remained. Early in the year 1800 he decided to restrict the number of Paris newspapers, whose ability to inform the public he further reduced by forbidding them to treat a great many subjects—

so that, muzzled when not abolished, the press lost much of its interest for readers. In general, cried the Emperor to Fouché in 1809, "the newspapers are always ready to grab at anything that can damage the public peace!" This declaration was soon followed by the creation of censors attached to each paper, and then by the draconian measures of 1810-1811: limitation of the number of journals of general information to four for Paris and one per department; confiscation of Paris newspapers and their assignment to companies controlled by the police. These measures had been preceded, moreover, by the establishment of new regulations for the printing trade, and had a precedent from the early days of the Consulate in the supervision over the theater.

No régime could be further than the Napoleonic from any respect for opinion, not opinion in the sense of support or disaffection among the popular masses, to which the regime was on the contrary very sensitive, but opinion as expressed by the enlightened element in the civic body, which might attempt to interpose between the government and these masses, to control the action of government by criticism, or to orient and orchestrate a mass reaction. Plebiscitary democracy simply passed over representative institutions and inhibited the development of public opinion. This was one aspect, among others, of the fundamental opposition between Napoleonic France and its British adversary, and of the hostility of bourgeois liberalism to the new régime, a liberalism incarnated, not without courage, by Benjamin Constant.

As for the liberty of persons, Jacques Godechot observes that the loss of it dated from well before 18 Brumaire—it was a matter in which the revolutionaries lacked the leisure to reconcile principles and practice—and that in 1814 there were only 2,500 persons arbitrarily confined in the state prisons. We should add, nevertheless, that the system of supervised residence, a restraint on individual liberty in the name of security of the State, was widely used by the prefects to isolate militant minorities, especially the former Jacobins and terrorists.

In any case, the police-state character of the Napoleonic régime is apparent. While it was an innovation to have a Ministry of Police, in which Fouché for so long distinguished himself, the importance and effectiveness of the police role were not new, especially in Paris:

Jean Tulard notes that the prefecture of police took over its institutional form from the Old Régime, and inherited from the Directory the files and the methods of its Central Bureau. We know, too, that Napoleon counted for the excellence of his police work on competition among his agents, those of Fouché, those of Dubois, and his own, not to mention the bits of information that he collected himself in his audiences, his chance encounters, and his correspondence. It is disquieting to see this primordial interest that Napoleon took in his police apparatus. Necessary in the troubled political atmosphere of the time, indispensable for the security of a rapidly rising personal power, having to its credit some remarkable pieces of detection, it nevertheless stands as evidence of the fragile basis of the consular and imperial system. Before Napoleon, only the Habsburg monarchy had given the police such a favored place.

The Executive

Eighteen Brumaire and the Constitution of the Year VIII signified fundamentally, though not formally, the reestablishment of a certain kind of monarchy. In this sense, the Babouvist Sylvain Maréchal was a good prophet when he put these words into the mouth of Bonaparte, Commanding General of the Army of Italy: "People of France! I will compose a Legislative Body and an Executive Directory for you! I will give you a king of my own design!" If we may believe Miot de Melito, Bonaparte as early as 1797 let it be understood that he considered outdated the kind of regime that had tried to replace the feeble Louis XVI: "Do you suppose that it is for a republic that I am winning victories in Italy? What an idea! A republic of thirty millions! It is a notion that the French are infatuated with, but it will pass like so many others." Buonarroti, in writing of Bonaparte in 1828, "He gave the coup de grace to the Revolution," echoed the *Considerations on the French Revolution* of Mme de Staël: "It was the first time since the Revolution that a person's name was on everyone's lips. Until then it was said: 'The Constituent Assembly has done such-and-such, or the people, or the Convention'; now the talk was all about this man who was going to put himself in the place of all others, and render the human race anonymous by monopolizing celebrity for himself."

But if it is true that Bonaparte forced his way sword in hand, it is false to say that he replaced the failing Directory with a military dictatorship, as the Babouvists had predicted. "Of all military men he is the most civilian," said Sieyès. Military glory was prerequisite for the success of his *coup de force*, the guarantee of the rapid extension of his powers accepted with hardly a murmur, and in the end the unfulfilled condition for the survival of his empire. In short, if war and the army were in the final analysis inseparable from the history of the Consulate and Empire, they were nevertheless only auxiliary to an experience in which the general was clearly effaced by the Chief of State. One of the most certain dangers for Napoleon Bonaparte was precisely the support given by other generals to various conspiracies, to which they rallied from jealousy at not having been invited to a real share in power after Brumaire, far more than from actual ideological principles.

What then was at issue? Not at all a classical monarchy, analogous to that of the fallen Bourbons, with which the rupture at bottom continued to be very definite. Nor was it a new version of the collegial executive dear to the revolutionary regimes: although there were three consuls in the Year VIII, the decision of the First Consul alone was sufficient (article 42); and his preeminence was signified by the enormous difference in their salaries, 500,000 as against 150,000 francs. What was at issue was a new kind of power, which indeed came out of events since 1789—Bonaparte is the great parvenu of the Revolution—but which even more was the embodiment in a strong personality of a philosophical ideal never attempted either by the politico-social Old Régime or by the successive institutions of the Revolution. Writing in 1791, Cabanis had interpreted the ideas of Mirabeau, recently deceased: "He thought that the liberty gained by insurrection should be preserved by respect for the laws; that the laws needed an active force to be executed; and that in a large empire whose people were not yet enlightened, and whose habits and attitudes have been degraded by centuries of slavery, this active force could only rest in the hands of one man."[1] This meant concentration of an expanded authority in new hands, those of a man committed to the modernization of the State and society. In effect, with reservations for the arbitrary and brutal methods that were so disappointing to Cabanis and his friends, this was the spirit of the Brumaire regime. It was "an alliance of de-

mocracy and authority," in René Rémond's definition of Bona-
partism, to which it may be added that the democracy was passive,
and only the authority active.

This new sovereign for which there was not yet a word was not
a Merovingian king but a man of the Enlightenment. For the exercise
of his authority he surrounded himself with many men and institutions to inform and assist him—auxiliaries all the more indispensable since the master had a taste for supervising all details. We
shall see later the variety of individual and political destinies among
the Napoleonic personnel, recruited, as Molé said, on the sole criterion of aptitude and talent. First we must note the essential role
of the Council of State, an appointed body, in the technical preparation of texts submitted to the deliberations of the Tribunate and
the Legislative Body, but also, paradoxically, in the basic political
life of these years. In a political life so restricted and often secret,
the role of the Council of State was of especial importance, although
we can find out little about it. It was within this "aulic" institution
that Bonaparte and Napoleon allowed the fullest expression of
disagreement and even of opposition. Like the senators, the State
councillors were paid 25,000 francs a year, a sure sign of their place
in the hierarchies of servants of the Napoleonic régime. It was in
the special sections of the council—legislation, interior, finance, war
and navy—as also in its plenary sessions, that all the reforms and
codifications were worked out, at a tempo that slowed down in
proportion as the work was accomplished, but with the prestige of
the institution remaining unimpaired. In addition, the Council of
State was represented, along with the consuls, ministers, senators
and finally the grand dignitaries, in the private councils that were
held for special purposes after the Year X, for discussion of major
constitutional or diplomatic actions.[2]

At the level of execution the ministers came directly below the
emperor. Theirs was an ambiguous situation, for although their will
and signature were equivalent to Napoleon's and placed them very
high in the State, they had very little autonomy or power of decision,
as Charles Durand has shown; their personal opinions were not
supposed to prevail—and the same was true at the level of the
prefects. The councils of ministers were only meetings of individual
agents presenting reports and submitting proposals. Any one of

them had a better chance to play a direct advisory role with the First Consul, or later Emperor, by sitting on one of the special administrative boards, as in the case of Chaptal, who after 1810 sat permanently on the special board for commerce and manufacturers. On these boards, also, we find again representatives of the special sections of the Council of State, whose jurisdiction thus asserted itself at several levels. In addition, we shall soon see the mission of the Council of State in the practical training of young men slated to occupy the higher positions in all branches of the administration.

Did such an executive power have any strength apart from the person of Napoleon himself? The question arises as much for the higher civilian administration as for the military general staff. "We are all used to being led step by step, and don't know how to formulate grand designs," admitted Decrès, the Minister of Marine. Charles Durand speaks of the "weakness of the system under abnormal circumstances." In particular, when the regency council had to function in dramatic circumstances at the end of the winter of 1813-1814, the fact that Napoleon had no real political lieutenant was felt all the more cruelly because of the betrayals that were in the air. Such a situation surely affected the conditions that brought him to defeat and abdication.

From the Consulate to the Empire

It is easy to understand the logic and mechanism of a centralized personal power. More puzzling are the dynastic and regressive forms in which this power clothed itself after 1804, with the proclamation of the hereditary Empire and the ceremony of 2 December beneath the vaults of Notre-Dame.

The passage to imperial monarchy may be interpreted in terms of individual and family psychology. The appetite for power, as well as the taste for appearance and ostentation, are easy to see as early as the years 1800-1801. Bonaparte preferred the Tuileries of the kings to the Luxembourg of the Directors. He wore a red coat, a form of court dress, and the Regent diamond adorned his sword. He soon busied himself in reviving some elements of the "households" of the old monarchy, and of its etiquette. As for his own family, he felt as a Corsican the sentiments of solidarity and the duties of "the son who has succeeded." The family repaid him with a jealousy and a greed that was often petty; on the day of the coronation the Emperor's sisters refused to bear Josephine's ceremonial train. She was the creole whose fault was in being outside the clan. The family likewise pressed from early in the Consulate for a dynastic and monarchical transformation. Fontanes, one of the regulars in the Catholic and reactionary salon of Elisa Bonaparte, wrote in 1800 a *Parallel between Caesar, Cromwell, Monk and Bonaparte*: "Happy the Republic if he were immortal! . . . If suddenly Bonaparte were to be missing from his country, where would his heirs be? Where are the institutions that might carry on his examples or perpetuate his genius? The fate of thirty million depends on the life of one man!" Lucien Bonaparte, as Minister of the Interior, and as a candidate for a possible succession, thought it well to circulate this text as an anonymous pamphlet. This false maneuver at a time when the Consulate was still precarious led to his replacement by Chaptal.

But it is in political needs that we find the true meaning of the legitimation and consecration of the coup d'état of Brumaire five years later. It emerges from a two-fold assessment of the internal situation of France, and of its relations with the other independent states of Europe. Here we depart from the domain of mere institutions.

2. The Politics of Power

Napoleon Bonaparte and Royalism: Rallies and Ruptures

Historians should beware of false symmetries and balances where the two sides are not even. The victor of Brumaire did not follow a narrow path between two equally steep precipices, and the stabilization of the Republic was not threatened equally by Jacobins and by counterrevolutionaries. The latter were the only real danger, even though Brumaire was brought about by raising the specter of a return to the Commune and the Terror. The cadres of the "left," decimated or closely watched, were in no position to mobilize the urban popular masses, which had entered for the time being into a cycle of passivity. On the "right," on the other hand, Bonaparte had to face not only the hostility of the faithful of the Catholic Church but the civil war in the west and the machinations of the émigrés. Despite a hatred that one can only call sanguinary for the "Jacobins," that is, the former terrorists and Babouvists, Bonaparte spent his most arduous efforts in drawing the Revolution out of the impasse to which it had been brought by the rallying of important minorities to the counterrevolution.

If nevertheless the impression still prevails of an equivalence between a "right" and a "left" in the first days of the Consulate, it is due to certain pronouncements of the First Consul and the Brumairians, inspired by propaganda—or by illusion. Thus Napoleon to Joseph: "What revolutionary will not have confidence in an order where Fouché will be a minister? What gentleman will not hope to be able to live under the former bishop of Autun?" Or Cabanis, author of an *Adresse aux Français* of 19 Brumaire, issued in the name of the Five Hundred and the *Anciens*: "Royalism will not again raise its head. The hideous traces of revolutionary government will be effaced."

But let us compare the measures of "appeasement" taken toward each. As for the "left," members of revolutionary committees deported in the Year III were repatriated. The holiday of 14 July was retained as suited to encourage unity among republicans. The death of George Washington provided Bonaparte with the occasion for a eulogy of liberty. These were limited gestures considering the steps taken with a view to the "right." The coup d'état was followed immediately by substantial measures of relaxation toward moderate and counterrevolutionary minorities whom it was important to detach from royalism, if royalism was to be isolated and crushed. The law of hostages against the relatives of émigrés was abrogated on 22 Brumaire. The "Fructidorized" moderates were allowed to return, except Pichegru. The observance of 21 January as a holiday (celebrating the death of Louis XVI) was suppressed, and the oath of hatred for royalty was replaced by an oath of fidelity to the Constitution, which allowed priests to perform religious services freely, safe against the risk of deportation.

Most striking, however, is the importance that the First Consul attached to a political settlement of the religious question, beyond the mere reopening of the churches. Since 1796 Bonaparte had wished to treat with the Pope, to undo the error made by the Revolution in its attempt to regulate the status of the Church of France without the authority of the Holy See. But interfering with this realism, this refusal to govern against the believers and their clergy, was the difficulty of finding a common language with the papacy. To "reestablish religion" might be a political act in Paris, by a man as little embarrassed by scruples as by protocol, but it was above all a spiritual act at Rome, where after ten years of schism and persecution there was an extreme sensitivity of both feeling and language.

Bonaparte lost no time in ordering solemn obsequies for Pius VI, who had just died at Valence, but he could of course do nothing before the election of a successor. It was a piece of double good fortune that the new Pope, Pius VII, the bishop of Imola, was known to Bonaparte and esteemed by him, and that he was intelligent and bold enough to overcome, on this occasion, the scruples of his conscience and the hesitation aroused by his deep personal spirituality. It is highly significant that Bonaparte waited until ten days after the victory of Marengo to suggest to an Italian prelate his intention to negotiate, for he meant to conduct any negotiation only from a position of strength. For this reason he also insisted on transferring the discussions to Paris, where, during an interminable series of deals and bargains, punctuated by spectacular incidents, he even resorted to police surveillance, an ultimatum, and military threats.

In this Concordat, in which the abbé Bernier and the papal Secretary of State, Cardinal Consalvi, "erased and reerased every word" (as Monseigneur Leflon has put it), Rome seems to have made immense sacrifices. The first advantage won by the First Consul was to seal, by the very act of signing an agreement, the recognition of the French Republic by the Holy See, and hence the rupture of the traditional alliance between Rome and the legitimate monarchies. It was a disastrous blow to French royalism in exile, for it freed the faithful in the interior from scruples about the regime of the Year VIII. The second advantage was to confirm a church of salaried public servants, amenable to the State and having mainly sociological functions. Here we see a continuation of the Gallican tradition, but also of the thought of *philosophes* who had urged both the submission of the clergy to the State and its integration within it. The refusal to reestablish the religious orders meant also the rejection of any ecclesiastical life that might escape the authority of the bishops. Even the cathedral chapters were reduced to decorative functions. Thirdly, no question was raised about the sale of the former Church properties, a matter of great importance for strengthening the prestige of Bonaparte in the eyes of the property-owning segments of French society.

Pius VII, for his part, failed to obtain the recognition of Catholicism as the state religion. He agreed to use his authority for what Consalvi called "the massacre of a whole episcopate," by requiring the resignation of all French bishops, both constitutional and refractory, since Napoleon judged such a step to be indispensable for effacing all traces of the revolutionary schism. It is right to see in this operation an encouragement to ultramontanism, for it affirmed the powers of the Pope over the French Church. But it also encouraged a tendency in the French episcopate, that is, a whole ecclesiological movement for appeal to an ecumenical council in matters of discipline. This showed itself in the national council of 1811, when Napoleon, in conflict with the Pope, wished to transfer the canonical investiture for vacant sees to the metropolitan bishops, and the bishops responded by references to the Church Universal. Pius VII, finally, met defeat and humiliation with the Organic Articles published along with the Concordat by Bonaparte's unilateral action. These signified an ultra-Gallican conception of Church-State relations, worthy of Louis XIV, and reassured those in the Church who complained of the political opportunism of the Concordat. Among the numerous provisions of the Articles we may point out those that legalized all forms of worship in France, and those that strictly subordinated the lower clergy to the bishops ("prefects in violet robes"): only a fifth of the parish priests received the title of *curé*, and with it secure tenure; all others became simple *desservants* of *succursales*, that is assistant pastors.

What then did the Pope gain in this Concordat, "more likely to raise difficulties than to solve them" (Bernard Plongeron)? Maintenance of the unity of the Roman Church, which a consolidation of the schism in France might have ruined forever; recognition of canonical investiture, which allowed the Pope to overcome the ze-

lanti among the cardinals who opposed the Concordat but favored a reinforcement of spiritual authority; and resumption of regular pastoral life in France, where the new administrative and social status of the priest encouraged a growing number of ordinations, which reached several hundred by the end of the Empire.

Pius VII in any case remained attached to the results accomplished, a fact that deprived the small "shadow church" opposed to the Concordat of the possibility of resistance. His continuing attitude was shown later in his willingness to come to Paris for the Emperor's coronation. With the negotiation of the Concordat went the removal in October 1800 of 52,000 persons from the list of émigrés, of whom nothing was asked except fidelity to the Constitution. It was made clear to them that restitution of their property would be limited to what was still unsold by the administration of the national domain. The success of this policy was assured by the attitude of the émigrés, who had begun to return discreetly immediately after the coup d'état and before any arrangement in their favor. To return did not mean to rally actively, but in any case it accentuated the isolation of the Bourbon pretender among a minority of irreconcilables, who were obliged to wait for 1814-1815, while pursuing their struggle against Napoleon Bonaparte from outside the country.

Their existence, however, and their connections in France, explain why Bonaparte's policy toward royalism took on the character of police repression while at the same time being conciliatory in its general principles. Toward those who persisted in seeing in him nothing but a usurper or a tool of others, the First Consul made use of violence, both verbal and physical, while he wiped out the past for those who—with a little surveillance—would make formal allegiance to his person. From Brumaire to the coronation there were several times when he burned his bridges or shed blood. The truce with the Vendéans did not prevent him from having Frotté put to death, despite the immunity normally granted to a negotiator. The victory of Marengo, "baptism of Napoleon's personal power," allowed him to reply to an approach from Louis XVIII in a cutting and haughty letter. In 1804 several executions followed the Cadoudal trial, and then came the condemnation to death of the duc d'Enghien, accomplished both by arbitrary seizure and by a claim to legality. There were other executions under the Empire in 1808-1809.

But while the transition from the Republic to the Empire was achieved without bloodshed (it had been prepared two years earlier by Napoleon's becoming Consul for Life, which still did not adequately reflect the real powers he already held), it nevertheless was an important break with the past. In a brilliant maneuver Napoleon, not content with testing the stability of his system by plebiscitary democracy to get the hereditary principle accepted, obtained the presence of the Pope himself at his coronation, on conditions almost as mortifying to the pontiff as those of the Concordat, and thus Bonaparte transferred to his own person whatever was left of respect and affection for legitimate monarchy. "What a defeat for the Bourbons!" observes Charles Durand. "The reactions of the comte de Lille* and of Joseph de Maistre showed the force of the blow thus struck at many Catholic consciences." Royalism, isolated inside France, was now isolated outside it as well, since the regime of Brumaire was now assimilated to the traditional European states in symbolic forms, though remaining in ideological conflict with them.

The best way then to prevent the return of the Old Régime, according to Napoleon, was to borrow its attractions. Such borrowing could not be convincing to partisans of a republic which, though imperial, was the daughter of the equalitarian Revolution. Too many fripperies recalling memories that were all too recent were again being honored. We get the impression that henceforth the Napoleonic regime was somehow "frozen," as the Revolution had been frozen after the great trials of the Year II. A visitor today can sense the chill in the small gallery of portraits at the Bois-Préau museum at Malmaison, where busts by Canova and paintings by Gérard are assembled, images of a family doing what it could to live up to the official art of an imperial court. There is the same impression of artificiality in the search for historical references other than those of the Capetians—the Roman Empire, the Carolingian Empire; and in the choice of emblems—the eagle, the laurel crown, the bee; or indeed the site of the coronation, Notre-Dame in Paris.

* The Comte de Lille was the courtesy title of the future Louis XVIII at this time; Joseph de Maistre was the famous counter-revolutionary writer. (Trans.)

To accept all this there had to be a sensibility blunted by fifteen years of vast and unexpected upheavals. And also a careful psychological preparation: several months of travel throughout the country, and at Boulogne-sur-Mer a massive distribution of medals to the army.

Napoleon Bonaparte and the "Interests"

In his great effort to rally moderates to his person, was Napoleon as successful in soothing the economic interests as in pacifying religious and political consciences?

Albert Vandal could present the Consulate as "a succession of Edicts of Nantes." We can extend the analogy, and speak of a Concordat of *rentiers*. The decree of 23 Thermidor VIII (11 August 1800) announced that from the second half of the Year VIII annuities and interest would be paid in specie. A medal was struck for the occasion, bearing the legend, *Fides publica. Foenus stata die solutum* (Public trust. Payment of interest when due). The Consolidated Third, which stood at only 11 francs on 18 Brumaire, went above 30 after Marengo, then reached 50, and even 60—an altogether exceptional rise. On 20 Floréal X the Consolidated Third was renamed the Consolidated Five Percent, and payments were to be made within a month after maturity by a prior claim on the revenues of the real property tax.

In a society such as the French, with its passion for acquiring land, it was politically necessary also to consolidate the various properties nationalized in the Revolution, and to remove the differences between real estate that was privately owned and that which was in the national domain. The land market had become sluggish with a tendency to fall, so far as sales from the national domain were concerned, because of fears aroused by the return of the émigrés, despite all official promises. The Concordat provided formal guarantees. Yet a theoretical danger remained on the hypothesis that the counterrevolution might triumph. Bonaparte could give total satisfaction to the new owners only in so far as he might combine military victory with a general and definitive peace. This was precisely what the Consulate and Empire failed to accomplish.

The problem of a "return to normalcy," to the situation before 1792, was also the main problem for business people of all kinds, except for those concerned with military supplies. Internal stabilization was in itself an inestimable advantage for them. We see a sign of it in the enthusiasm of a Paris banker, Barrillon, in a letter written to his colleague Greffulhe of London: "Then came the 18 Brumaire and Bonaparte: with a government mending the situation, there was a lifting of spirits and everyone expected internal peace and a rosier future; there were new ideas, and the face of things changed."[3] But in general no particular solicitude was shown for the bankers, merchants and manufacturers, either in their current affairs or in economic policy as a whole. Their interests were subordinated to a foreign policy that obeyed its own logic. Representatives of the great economic interests were part of the sectors of opinion that became progressively detached from the regime. The security it offered was simply not adequate.

Napoleon Bonaparte and the "Left"

Finally, the character of the Napoleonic regime becomes evident in its attitudes toward the liberal and Jacobin opposition. As Buonarroti wrote later in his *Conspiracy for Equality*: "The new aristocracy was bound to see in this general the man who would one day give them solid support against the people; and knowing his aristocratic opinions and haughty nature, they appealed to him, on the 18 Brumaire of the Year VIII, when they were frightened by the rapid reappearance of the democratic spirit." Bonaparte, in whose eyes the worst fault of Louis XVI had been to compound with the rioters on the memorable day of June 20, 1792, Bonaparte the enemy of government by the street, undoubtedly felt a profound hatred for the old "terrorists," a hatred that was systematic to the point of blindness. The proof is in the use he made of the attempted assassination in the rue Saint-Nicaise. He decided instantly to attribute it to the Jacobins and Babouvists, and announced his attention to set an example. "We will not spare blood," he said in the Council of State, and he told Roederer, "I have a dictionary of the September murderers, conspirators, Babeuf and others who figured at the worst moments of the Revolution." When Fouché, after a two-week investigation, brought in proof that the attempt was the work of royalists, Bonaparte became obstinate and insisted on a list of proscriptions to punish the militant Jacobins for their political past—"for 2 September, 31 May, the conspiracy of Babeuf, and all that has happened since," according to Thibaudeau. The matter ended with the *senatus-consulte* of 15 Nivôse of the Year IX (5 January 1801), deporting 130 persons as "a measure to preserve the Constitution."

The same program of elimination, by methods that were more humane though no less arbitrary, struck at the first signs of parliamentary opposition. In 1802 the Tribunate was purged by the Senate when the time came for a fifth of its membership to be retired by lot. Then it saw itself fragmented into three sections—Legislation, Interior and Finance—without the right to sit together as a full assembly. The suppression the next year of the class in moral and political sciences of the Institute completed the destruction of centers of independent political thought. Various arrests, and the removal of officers and troops suspected of republican disaffection all pointed in the same direction, and was one reason for the expedition to Saint-Domingue, which neutralized the Army of the Rhine.

The consular and imperial power was in short a power that defended itself by attacking. But if fundamentally the new power was so rapidly established, aided by the prestige of military victory, it was because its active opponents were only minorities. On the whole the struggle against them hardly interested the bulk of the population. It did not oblige Bonaparte to multiply his acts of violence and his victims indefinitely. Even better, thousands of men with administrative abilities, coming from a wide variety of backgrounds, and under new institutional arrangements, consented to serve the First Consul whose authority they recognized and admired. Bonaparte had the elites on his side. To make a brief inventory of them is doubtless the best way to analyze the conditions under which the new regime could be effective.

II

⚬꙳꙳꙳⚬

A Country under
Administrative Tutelage

Was the system inherited, or newly invented? Insofar as political
forms are concerned we can give a guarded answer in favor of its
novelty, for the means of access to public office and the constitutional principles and habits that had been developing under the
Directory were quickly forgotten or dissolved in a new style for the
exercise of power and in the establishment of a new legitimacy.

But in administrative institutions it is continuity that should be
stressed. Directed by a stronger hand, sometimes given new names,
supplemented by a few new creations at both the lower and intermediate levels, these institutions are still easily recognizable: the
tradition of the Old Régime in the days of its reforming efforts, the
attempted recentralization under the Convention and the Directory
after the earlier reforms of the Constituent Assembly, came together
in the establishment of an administrative "grid," which, though
indeed rationalized and simplified, seemed to express a spirit that
existed both before and after the Revolution, and to operate through
a personnel whose legal status changed more than the men themselves.[1]

1. THE PREFECTS

The prefects in charge of the *départements*, with their subprefects
created when the *arrondissements* were restored, call to mind even
today, and in one word, the omnipresence and uniformity of a
central authority jealous of its prerogatives.

It is impossible to study them without noting the character of the
administration in Paris that directed them. This was the powerful

DEPARTMENTS OF THE FRENCH EMPIRE ABOUT 1810

France within its pre-Revolutionary borders (shown by the heavy line) was reorganized by the Constituent Assembly in 1789-1791 into eighty-three departments. The First Republic added not only Alpes Maritimes, Mont-Blanc and Léman, which form part of France today (the latter two now called Savoie and Haute-Savoie), but also the area of Belgium and the Left Bank of the Rhine. Parts of Italy and northwest Germany, and the whole Dutch territory, followed under Napoleon, until by 1810 there were 130 departments, each under its prefect.

Ministry of the Interior—the only ministry that counted, along with that of Police, which was distinct from it in 1800-1801 and again from 1804 to 1814. Since 1790 the Ministry of the Interior had taken over most functions of the pre-Revolutionary controller-general of finance and the old Royal Household. Broken up into twelve executive commissions by the dictatorship of the Committee of Public Safety, reestablished as a ministry in the Year IV, strongly marked by the personality of François de Neufchâteau, it received a precise and disciplined organization from the men to whom Napoleon Bonaparte entrusted it: first his brother Lucien, the only one who brought to it a true political sense; and then to Chaptal, Champagny, Crétet and Montalivet, who were industrious and amenable high-level clerks. An amazing array of activities depended on the Interior: in addition to municipal and "general" administration (population, conscription, the national guard) there were agriculture, subsistences, commerce, "arts and manufactures" (these last two becoming a separate ministry from 1811 to 1814), public assistance, prisons, the great artistic and scientific institutions, public works, Mines, Roads and Bridges, public instruction, the archives . . . and statistics. In contrast, the functions of Justice, Finance, the Treasury, War, Navy, Colonies and Foreign Relations seem narrowly specialized. We can hardly comprehend today how such a "machine," which seemed such a ponderous bureaucracy to contemporaries, was manned by hardly more than two hundred persons, from the minister and his secretary-general down to the messengers and office boys, with division chiefs, bureau chiefs, under-chiefs, scribes, clerks and despatchers in between. As Montalivet explained in his *General Instructions* of 1812, "the center must know whatever is being done, for good or ill. . . . We must have analyses that show what is done or not done on every matter, the way in which things are done in different places and at different times." It is understandable that the Ministry of the Interior, "the State's memory" to use another expression of Montalivet's, had as a principal function the conducting of a gigantic correspondence with all points of the empire, a mass of paper-work that was constantly fed by the growing minuteness of the regulations.*

* For a list of ministers and ministries under Napoleon, see pp. 73-76 below.

ADMINISTRATIVE SEATS

The map shows the town in each department where the prefect had his office, the prefecture. Towns whose names are in all-capital letters are those which had both a prefecture and an appellate court, there being one such court for about every four departments. The few towns whose names are in italics are those where the appellate court was in a different place from the prefecture.

Depository of these multiple functions, and privileged partner in those epistolary exchanges, was the prefect. Not, indeed, that he was supposed to exercise any power whatsoever. In both directions, between the government and the people administered, he was expected to be perfectly transparent and neutral, assuring the execution of orders and the transmission of information. He was more an agent than an associate of unusual talents. "They have no right to proclaim either their will or their opinions" (Lucien Bonaparte). "The chain of execution descends without interruption from the minister to the administration, and transmits the law and the orders of government into the farthest ramifications of the social order with the speed of the electric fluid" (Chaptal).

If the uniform that he wore hardly promised him the joys of a proconsulship, it required of the prefect singular qualities of devotion, observation and flexibility and a certain aptitude for incarnating authority. "Your powers," said one of the first circulars of Lucien Bonaparte, "embrace everything that relates to the public fortune, national prosperity, and tranquillity of the people over whom you are charged with the administration." That is to say, beyond overall supervision of the various administrative sections, except the military, the prefect's mission was political in the broad sense. The First Consul counted on his prefects to transmit the image of a recuperative regime into daily life. They were therefore first of all responsible for local order, which was no longer to be troubled by the quarrels, henceforth things of the past, between partisans and adversaries of the Revolution. Emigrés whether amnestied, de-listed or simply returning; old Jacobins and "terrorists"; artisans who met secretly to sing the Marseillaise or celebrate the Tenth of August; independent spirits such as notaries, lawyers or literary men; meetings of clubs, academies, lodges—all were subjects of preoccupation, investigation, assembly of files, and drafting of reports on "public opinion."

It was necessary also to assure the conditions for enforcement of the great measures of pacification, which might impose very disagreeable obligations on the population. Thus in the case of the Concordat the installation of new curés ran the risk of reviving conflicts centering about the former constitutional or refractory priests; in the payment of taxes, and notably the united excise, the procedures of collection could lead to incidents in the wine-growing departments when inventories of the vintage were required, as in the former province of Burgundy, which had been exempt from excises at the end of the Old Régime; and naturally in the matter of conscription, when draft evasion and desertion had to be dealt with. It was an unfortunate prefect whose department embraced vast wooded areas, as in the Yonne, where Bléneau, a man of the old monarchy, considered the inhabitants of the canton of Quarré-les-Tombes to be "half savages." A prefect in any case hesitated to use repression, both because such action might lead those in higher quarters to think his administration unsuccessful, and because the use of force would make his later relations with the population more difficult. Nevertheless Méchin, the prefect of Caen, in 1812, faced with grain riots at the end of the winter, felt obliged to submit a report that induced the Minister of Police, Savary, to send 4,000 men to the Calvados in support of court-ordered enforcement meant to serve as an example.

The work of a prefect also had its more positive aspects. He had to prepare for installation of the new administrative structures by finding persons suited for employment, according to their family, their fortune, their abilities or their opinions; hence the importance of "moral and personal statistics." It was his duty to preside at expressions of political life, which in truth became more summary and infrequent—the plebiscites, swearing of oaths, establishment and revision of the lists of most highly taxed citizens and of members of electoral colleges. He had sometimes to make arrangements for visits by the First Consul or Emperor. Finally, it was incumbent on him to follow and encourage all forms of economic life. A circular of Lucien Bonaparte recommended: "To promote peace in your department, divert toward notions of political economy what is left of the restlessness that follows a great revolution." For the economy a first prerequisite was public security. Food supply remained a continuing problem, especially in a department that habitually or occasionally had a deficit in grain. Everywhere the prefect watched over provisioning of the markets, the free circulation of grains, and their prices (reported fortnightly by arrondissement), while also making forecasts of the harvest. In a crisis he might take exceptional measures, reminiscent of the "police" of the Old Régime and the

Terror: mandatory declaration of stocks of flour and grain, under penalty of domiciliary visits; requisitions on farmers and grain merchants, enforced by the gendarmerie if necessary; importation when needed from departments having a surplus; mandatory sale in the public marketplace at a fixed price; prohibition to cut grain before full maturity; setting the date for beginning the harvest, etc.

No less regularly, the prefects, created at a time when demographic and economic statistics, for better or worse, were finding a place in the central administrations, spent much of their energy and talent—or that of their collaborators, notably the secretaries-general of the prefectures—in replying to the most varied and extensive questions proposed by the Minister of the Interior. The political report, the statistical memoir and the "statement of the situation" figure among the most representative pieces of prefectoral "literature." "Established facts are the sole principles of the sciences," Condillac had said; and it was in this spirit that Lucien Bonaparte and his successors wanted to base the action of government on exact and positive knowledge. Some prefects, such as Beugnot, prefect of the Seine-Inférieure from 1800 to 1806, threw themselves with a passion into acquiring a most intimate understanding of the activities of their department. There was nothing that Beugnot did not know about the techniques, machines, men, wages, capital investments, selling prices, and conditions of international competition concerning the textile industry and associated activities of the region of Rouen and the Pays de Caux. His zeal, paradoxically, prevented him from ever completing his departmental statistics, which were so excessively well prepared!

In short, the prefecture could be occupied either by a dull but irreproachable personage, or, on the contrary, thanks to the important margin that it gave for local administrative initiative, it might call forth a kind of genius. In this category we should doubtless put the case of Adrien de Lezay-Marnésia, prefect of the Rhin-et-Moselle from 1806 to 1810, and of the Bas-Rhin from 1810 to 1814. This nobleman from the Jura, educated at the Brunswick Carolinum and the university of Göttingen, disciple of Rousseau and Pestalozzi, a half-hearted émigré inclined to favor a republic of propertyowners, was a man of the Enlightenment who rallied to Bonaparte after the peace of Lunéville. Though he began a diplomatic career as minister to Salzburg in 1803, he found his true vocation in departmental administration. "For any people, it is only by administration that the government can be loved. As goes the administration, so go the people administered." At Coblenz he put German Rhinelanders into positions of responsibility. At Strasbourg, at the end of the Empire, he remained the most liberal of the prefects; with "the impatience of a rationalist convinced of the rightness of his ideas" he created a normal school, encouraged smallpox vaccination, promoted the growth of crops needed for forage or industrial purposes, watched over the local roads by restoring a "corvée," and created cantonal commissioners—soon disavowed in Paris—who were prominent local citizens charged with touring the department to inform him on the state of opinion. Aiming at reform, liberty and public welfare, he was a man who believed that he found under Napoleon the conditions favorable to putting the social philosophy of the eighteenth century to work.

It is hard to reach a final judgment on the prefectoral administration and the growth of administrative centralization. Was Napoleon more abreast of the affairs of his empire, or better obeyed, than a Bourbon of the days of absolutism? He personally did all that he could to keep his functionaries under control, informing himself of their activity, removing them, rebuking them, or congratulating them even when he was campaigning at the other end of Europe. As the prefects made the rounds to inspect their subordinate municipalities, so Napoleon made the rounds of his departments, and these speedy visits seemed to him enough to correct on the spot any false perspectives raised by administrative prose.

Yet Montalivet was not so sure. "In general the prefects only report what they want to, and as they want to. What I see most clearly is that we know nothing of what is going on." At the other end of the chain Joseph Fiévée, a prefect himself, with an independent mind, criticized the nullity of prefectoral administration. "The mania for regulating everything from Paris down to the smallest details will inhibit the personal development of administrators, so that I am more convinced than ever of the rational impossibility of telling the difference between a good prefect and a bad one" (1810). "The blind force of any agent of a violent authority has been mistaken for administrative power, and this error will be fatal for administration. . . . " "I have had the honor of being a prefect, and I never claimed to direct public opinion in my department. I knew positively at the time that I was not directing the public opinion of my own antechamber." As Tocqueville and Royer-Collard were soon to point out after the Restoration, the Revolution and the Napoleonic dictatorship left nothing standing between a powerful central administration, with its clerks and deputies, and a pulverized dust of administered individuals.

At least Napoleon made a serious effort to replace the empiricism of his first appointments with a systematic training program for his future subprefects, prefects, magistrates and functionaries of all branches of the higher administration. It was for this reason, in 1803, that he created the auditors of the Council of State and constantly increased their numbers. By 1813 a quarter of the prefects had arrived by that route, and the way was open for a new generation of young men formed under the eyes of the master in the practical experience of affairs. It was an attractive channel of advancement for men of the comfortable bourgeoisie or old aristocracy, "the sons, sons-in-law and nephews of ministers, senators, state councillors, generals, prefects," and it was well calculated to rally families and form personal loyalties to the Emperor.

2. The Attempt to Control Society

Justice

Judicial reform, like the creation of the prefectures, was part of the set of great administrative measures introduced in the first months of the Consulate. There was less in it of comparable interest or novelty. It was especially in this area that the Napoleonic program consisted of readjustments of institutions devised by the Revolution, and in introducing details that had been overlooked and which were oddly reminiscent of the Old Régime. The work also revealed certain preoccupations that were natural for a régime aiming at order above all else.

Except for justices of the peace, whose numbers were later reduced, and for the judges in the tribunals of commerce, all judges were appointed. "You are appointed for life," Bonaparte wrote to them in May 1800. "No one has the right to remove you; you are responsible only to your consciences for your judgments; you are to be as impassive as the law." The First Consul thus meant to signify the role of the courts in the reestablishment and maintenance of civil peace. But as Charles Durand has noted, the limit to the judges' independence lay in the fact that the government controlled their advancement. It was the government that named those who were to preside on the bench, for limited terms.

Below the department level, in the chief town of each arrondissement, was a court of first instance combining civil and correctional jurisdiction. Above the department an appellate system was reestablished, with one court for four departments on the average. Their location followed that of the Parlements, sovereign courts, superior councils, tax courts and presidials of the monarchy, though they enjoyed far less prestige for various reasons. At first called tribunals, these appellate bodies later took the name of "courts," and the departmental *tribunal criminel* became a *cour d'assises*, echoing the old royal vocabulary.

The government added a clearly repressive feature to the judicial apparatus in the Year IX. To each court of first instance in the arrondissements it attached a deputy of the government commissioner associated with the departmental criminal court. These "security officers" were empowered to initiate prosecutions. Even more clear was the significance of the special courts that aroused such protest from the liberal opposition, and which undoubtedly made for a system of political and military justice, even though the purpose at first was to restore security on the roads and in the open country.

Education

Virtually from beginning to end of the consular and imperial period we can see Napoleon Bonaparte earnestly occupied with the reconstitution of a corporate teaching body. "My University," he was to say in 1815, "in the way that I conceived it, was a masterpiece of organization, and was to become one in its consequences for the nation." Elsewhere he often explained the close connection that he saw between schools and the stability of his political program. "There will be no settled political state," he said, "so long as there is not a teaching body with settled principles. So long as one does not learn from childhood whether to be republican or monarchist, Catholic or nonreligious, etc., the State will not form a nation; it will rest on a vague and uncertain base; it will be constantly exposed to changes and disorders" (1805).

Childhood, however, remained outside the new organization. Much primary teaching was scattered among private and confessional schools. In the public sector it was left as a responsibility of local municipalities and families. In the view of a society strongly hierarchized by property and money, what the "lower classes" needed, beyond a few "elementary notions," was only moral formation and good work habits. At this level there was nothing contradictory to official views in leaving control to the Catholic Church.

The Napoleonic regime did in truth encourage, though feebly, the development of popular technical instruction of which the drawing schools of the end of the Old Régime had been a first version. Chaptal and the Society for the Encouragement of National Industry, in which administrators, scientific men and business leaders were associated, recommended the multiplication of vocational schools, as likely both to be self-financing and to maintain social peace. At Paris Chaptal opened at the Conservatory of Arts and Trades a practical school of spinning and weaving (1804), which became a nursery for foremen in the textile industry, and Champagny added in 1806 a free school for draftsmen. In the provinces two Schools of Arts and Trades were opened at Châlons and at Beaupréau near Angers. The former, first installed at Compiègne, derived in part from a school opened in 1786 at Liancourt by the duke of La Rochefoucauld, who was made inspector-general of these establishments in 1806. "The inadequacy of measures of popular education and technical instruction," according to A. Léon, "reflected the contradictions in a society caught between attachment to the artisanal values of the Old Régime and a new consciousness of the needs of industrial development."[2]

The efforts of the Consulate and Empire were mainly expended on secondary instruction. This was an instruction meant for the sons of notables, and its purpose was to give them a general education to precede their specialized studies, which in turn consisted in professional training for administrative and liberal careers. So far as the general orientation thus impressed on French society is concerned, it is more important to analyze the content of this instruction than to find what use was made of the "products" of the forty-five lycées planned for in 1802. "In original temperament Napoleon was a romantic," says André Monglond, and as a young man he delighted in the *Nouvelle Héloïse*, the *Confessions* of Rousseau, *Paul and Virginia* and Ossian, but when he came to power he donned the mask of admiration for the age of Louis XIV, "and had the most classical culture distributed by the Imperial University." In fact, the work of the Consulate in this matter must be seen in context with the controversy since before 1800 over the Central Schools of the Directory, which had been strongly criticized both for their excessive liberalism in pedagogy and discipline, and for their unbalanced emphasis on the sciences. Even Cabanis, a man of science, thought early in the Year VIII that "literary instruction is the preliminary and indispensable basis of all others." A report of the Council on Public Instruction recommended the return to six years of compulsory Latin and four of Greek, but it appeared after the coup d'état and remained a dead letter. The situation favored a quasi-political offensive against the educational system produced by the Revolution. The Catholic and royalist reaction attacked the Republic and "philosophy" by attacking the Central Schools, and demanded the reestablishment of colleges of the humanities to be taught by men in religious orders. Chaptal was not far from yielding, being himself in favor of freedom for private schools. Such, however, was not Bonaparte's idea, which found expression in the plan drawn up by Fourcroy and enacted by the law of 11 Floréal of the Year X. The suppression of the Central Schools brought not the restoration of the old colleges but the establishment of the lycées as civil institutions of the State. The lycées revived the boarding facilities, the discipline, and the predominance of literary studies over the sciences, history and philosophy that had characterized the colleges before 1789. The recruitment of their professors was assured by revival of the *agrégation* in 1808.

The law of 10 May 1806, founding the University of France, defined it as "a body charged exclusively with public teaching and education in the whole Empire," having as its function "to direct political and moral opinions." Napoleon flattered himself on assuring its material independence with an endowment of 400,000 francs of annual income, to be supplemented by the payments of parents. The grand-master of the University, placed directly under orders of the minister, that is the Emperor, was a considerable personage who, aided by a chancellor and a council, stood at the summit of a new hierarchy as distinct as that of the prefectures, judicial districts and dioceses. Below him were the "academies," or geographical areas, in each of which authority "descended" from the rector through inspectors to the principals of schools. The nomination of Fontanes as first grand master confirmed the conservative spirit of the new teaching body.

The Napoleonic university included a level of higher education in the form of faculties—for medicine, law, theology, letters and sciences. But this level only developed step by step over the course of the nineteenth century. At first, the only faculties to prosper were those of law and medicine, which had existed as special schools before the establishment of the University. The faculties of letters and of sciences, with very limited numbers of professors, remained simple extensions of the lycées, and their teaching was hardly more advanced than in the higher lycée classes. Thus the eight professors of the Paris faculty of sciences were all borrowed from other institutions, and its general course in the sciences (there was a parallel general course in mathematics) dealt with matters as varied as physics, chemistry, mineralogy, geology, botany, zoology and physiology. The course in physics itself was not very specialized, dealing with both hydrostatics and electricity. In fact, the teaching of science at an advanced level went on outside the University, in the great establishments for which only the Revolution could claim the credit.

Among these establishments the most useful in the eyes of Napoleon Bonaparte was the Polytechnic, founded in 1794. Its function and objectives were redefined in a reform that coincided with the beginning of the Consulate, and which provided for competitive admissions (for which there was as yet no system of preparation) and for two years of study giving access to special schools (as of Mines, Artillery and Roads and Bridges) called schools of application, which in turn led to higher employment in the public military and civil services. Thanks to a small subsidy from the State the Polytechnic was open to the sons of poor families, and in its early years almost half the students were sons of peasants and artisans. But in 1804-1805 the character of the institution changed. Students were henceforth obliged to pay a boarding fee of 800 francs a year. Above all, the school shifted from being a great scientific establishment, in which Berthollet, for example, taught at the most advanced frontier of theoretical and applied chemistry, to being a military school, directed by Lacuée under the War Department. In 1811 it was decided that the best students should be graduated as military engineers. From 1811 to 1813 two hundred were channeled into the artillery.

On the other hand, the College of France and the Museum of Natural History, as pure establishments for teaching and research, developed as intellectual centers and even as arenas of scientific controversy. Their professors met also in the first class of the Institute, where they formed a brilliant constellation. The government expected of them also the benefit of certain consultations, either on practical questions or as contributions to its own glory.

The Church

The political meaning of the Concordat is well known. Its purpose, internally, was to enable Bonaparte to restore national cohesion, an impossible objective without the adherence of the Catholic clergy, as ten years of civil struggles had proved. We shall say no more on the most obvious aspects of this adherence. It reached its high point in docility with the publication of the Imperial Catechism in 1806, which put civic obligations on a par with those of religion, as if the Emperor were seated at the right hand of God. At the same time the celebration of a Saint-Napoléon's Day, 15 August, replaced that of the Assumption of the Virgin Mary, which had been a royal and national holiday since "the vow of Louis XIII." On an essential point, the acceptance of conscription, as R. Darquenne has recently remarked of the Belgian departments, the Church lent important support to the military policy of "the restorer of religion." Episcopal letters ordered a *Te Deum* of thanksgiving for the victory at Austerlitz, to be celebrated henceforth on the first Sunday of December: "The God of Powers and of Armies has raised Napoleon on a throne consecrated by victory." Other episcopal letters and pastoral instructions in the following years dealt explicitly with the blood levy. Conscripts should "regard their summons as that of God . . .

One's country is the Ark of the Covenant between the Sovereign and the people." So spoke the bishop of Tournai, whom Réal did not hesitate to compare to one of the Emperor's grenadiers. The time came when refractories and deserters were refused absolution.

We shall come back to the essential limits of this good will on the part of the clergy, and notably the episcopate. Meanwhile, more discreetly but effectively, the clergy found itself reinvested by the Napoleonic institutions, or rather by their shortcomings, with a partial control over education, thus regaining one of its principal functions in the society of the Old Régime. Sheltered by the law of 11 Floréal of the Year X, the Christian Brothers resumed their activity, reorganizing themselves around a center at Lyon, and winning the approval of the grand master for their new regulations in 1810. In the University, priests taught in the lycées and acted as principals, rectors, inspectors and members of the Council. Outside the University, above all, and despite its supposed monopoly, there were about a thousand private establishments, among which the seminaries, and the houses of the newly authorized feminine orders, received a large clientele of persons who disliked the imperial lycées. Napoleon tried to react against all this, in 1811, with a series of measures to restrict the freedom of private education, in which many of the teachers were ecclesiastics or former ecclesiastics. Among the institutions that the Emperor hoped to use in his attempt to subject minds and consciences, the Church thus appeared to be a very ambiguous ally. Conscious of the need of concessions to a power that had restored normal conditions for its pastoral ministry, it also made use of its revived social and juridical position to extend its influence beyond mere cooperation in maintaining public order. It moved toward a spiritual and ideological conquest that was awkward for the Napoleonic régime, rooted as that régime was, underneath its authoritarian character, in fidelity to 1789.

3. The Fiscal System and Its Agents

It may seem arbitrary to turn to taxation in a chapter devoted to administrative structures, but surely such is not the case in dealing with the régime of Napoleon.

In fact, the Consulate and Empire brought no new solution to

the problems of taxation, concerning either its sources or the distribution of the burden—nor yet of the problems of credit. In these
matters the balance is clearly negative, both because Napoleon
thought in terms of politics or of merely practical problems of the
treasury, and because the extraordinary circumstances of French
expansion in Europe made imagination unnecessary. The Napoleonic accomplishment in this matter belongs in the domain of
financial administration; it was a more rigorous application of net-
works already existing or taken from an altogether classical arsenal.
"The financial achievement of the Napoleonic years is summarized
in the creation of a good administrative instrument, which had been
lacking in the old monarchy."[3]

The Tax Burden and Its Structure

Bonaparte preserved intact the fiscal inheritance from the governments of the Revolution, that is, a system of direct taxation.

The tax on real estate, first of all, provided almost three-quarters
of the government's resources from direct taxes. It produced 240
million francs in 1813, or about as much as in 1791 when it was
created. Such stability was obviously inconsistent with the enlarge-
ment of the French frontiers and the strong and continuous rise of
land values. But it no less obviously corresponded to the wishes of
the notables, always opposed to whatever might restrict the free
enjoyment of their property.

At the same date, in 1813, only 10 percent of the proceeds of
direct taxation was brought in by the tax on personal property.
This was composed of a fixed sum (the personal charge) plus a
variable amount (above a base equal to the value of three days'
labor as determined in each department) which fell on the external
signs of wealth—rents paid, servants, horses, carriages, chimneys—
in short a sumptuary tax on movables. This tax was suppressed in
stages from 1803 to 1808 in towns having the *octroi*, or levy on
goods entering the town, which replaced it.

The tax on doors and windows and the *patente*, a license to
engage in a trade or business, together yielded less than 6 percent
of the direct taxes. We must add that the direct taxes were aug-
mented by the *centimes additionnels*, levied in each department to
meet its expenses, the expenses of local governments, the cost of

land registry, and the upkeep and construction of roads for which the departmental councils were responsible.

But the whole of direct taxes in 1813 constituted only 29 percent of total receipts. It need hardly be said that their inelasticity made them very unsuited to support a "policy of grandeur." The fiscal system therefore was soon inevitably extended. In Napoleon's mind, as Robert Lacour-Gayet has said, "the only quality of a good fiscal system was its yield. What had to be found were various taxes that were easy to apply and automatically productive. The indirect tax under these conditions became the ideal tax." Or to quote the language of the First Consul himself, it was necessary "to establish a large number of indirect taxes, whose very moderate rate could be raised in proportion to need." Neither recoiling against the unpopularity of restoration of such taxes, nor disdaining a kind of resurrection of the monarchy, Napoleon Bonaparte reintroduced between 1802 and 1810 duties on tobacco, liquor and salt and finally a monopoly in the manufacture, purchase and sale of tobacco. These "united excises" grew until their yield was quadrupled between 1806 and 1812. Total taxes on consumers' goods produced about a quarter of the government's receipts in 1813. A third great branch of the revenue completed the total: stamp taxes, registry taxes and customs duties.

Hence was built up a fiscal system whose principles were hardly different from those of the Old Régime, and which was to last until the First World War and the adoption of the income tax. But in this "technical compromise" between taxes on consumption and taxes on wealth and on *some* forms of income we can easily see two constants: a protected situation for industrial and commercial profit, and an aggravation of indirect taxation. As Jean Bouvier expresses it, "an X-ray of the fiscal system bequeathed by the First Empire to its successors reveals an arrangement well adapted to the growth of profit, hence to growth *tout court*," and on the other hand an anti-democratic fiscal structure.

Such as it was, the Napoleonic fiscal system was inadequate to cover expenses, especially after 1806. At that date the expenditures were about 700 million francs, and they went well over 1,000 million in 1812 and 1813. Meanwhile the receipts, though perceptibly rising, were well under 1,000 million at the end of the reign.

The deficit arose from the ever heavier share consumed by military needs, which increased from about 60 percent to 80 percent of the total. They rose from 462 million in 1807 to 817 million in 1813, and these figures are probably below the reality. The campaigns of Ulm and Austerlitz had hardly cost 60 million; the war in Spain, according to Mollien, cost 70 million a year, and the expedition to Russia more than 700 million for 1812. The solution found was both artificial and fatally easy: artificial—in that there was a swelling of revenues with the progressive expansion of the frontiers of the Empire (involving admittedly greater costs of administration), and that customs revenues rose as the blockade against England became geographically wider and more effective; easy—in that, on the principle that "war should support war," it did not have to be paid for by the French taxpayer until 1812.

The confiscations of feudal and crown properties, real and personal, in defeated countries; the spoils taken directly from the enemy; the war indemnities in money and in kind, "justified" by the right of conquest or provided for in imposed treaties of peace, not only covered the needs of the armies but produced considerable surpluses, to which Napoleon alluded when he asserted, "I brought over two thousand million in specie into France," or when he claimed, at St. Helena, that he had "left 400 million in the cellars of the Tuileries." This is not the place to examine the dramatic consequences, for countries "under the boot," of such blood-lettings as the 311 million extracted from Prussia after Jena. On the administrative level, the managers of the Extraordinary Domain, organized definitively by the *senatus-consulte* of 1810 (La Bouillerie, Defermon), and those of the finances of the Grand Army in conquered territories (Daru, Estève, Villemanzy) surely counted among the most remarkable higher civil servants to be formed by the Empire. We must remember also that the Extraordinary Domain served to balance certain deficits in the ordinary budget, and to finance a policy of prestige that included monuments, public works and encouragement for the arts, as well as a system of rewards for civilian and military services—donations which, whether modest or fabulous, were the means of a social differentiation in which the privileged could boast of not being a burden to their compatriots.

Toward the end, however, these hundreds of millions, perhaps more, thus levied on the vanquished fell toward zero as the French armies were pushed back into Western Europe.

The Refusal to Resort to Loans

In the difficult circumstances at the end of 1813 Napoleon was therefore driven to cover his expenses by enormous increases in the direct taxes, which must have been a far from negligible element in the rising political crisis that led to the vote for his deposition. Probably fearing to end in the way the Ancien Régime had perished, or unwilling to subject himself to control by opinion through the use of credit, both as Consul and then as Emperor he stubbornly refused to borrow. On problems of credit Lacour-Gayet observes that "his ideas were elementary, not to say primitive." They were inspired by a kind of petty-bourgeois morality (it was immoral to take assured future income in advance, and a fatal source of additional expense) and by a rigid sense of the dignity of the State, since the public power should not depend on bankers and merchants.

But the Consulate and Empire could not avoid the problem of credit insofar as they inherited, by way of the bankruptcy and reconsolidation effected under the Directory, what was left of the debt of the Old Régime. Eager to give reassurances and to liquidate the past, the government even agreed to enlarge the public debt derived from the "Consolidated Third" of the Directory by accepting responsibility for the arrears of the Directory after the peace of Lunéville in 1801, and by assuming the public debt of Holland after annexation of that country in 1810. The Five Percents, as the debt was now called, involved payments of interest that rose from 35 to 45 and finally 63 million francs a year.

But the respect for prior engagements was a purely political act, meant to produce confidence. It in no way signified an intention to resort to future borrowings. The concern for wiping out the arrears had the same implication. The market for government obligations was strictly organized and controlled. Dealing in them was confined to a small number of traders, named by the First Consul and obliged to give a security bond of 60,000 and later 100,000 francs. In Paris the sixty-odd authorized traders had grounds for complaining that their profits were trifling and derived from very small volume, the more so since a quarter of the debt was locked up in the hands of great public establishments.

The Refusal to Resort to Paper Money

The lesson of the Revolutionary money, buried under its own ruins, was as well remembered as the lesson of the Old Régime suffocated by its debts. Napoleon steadily refused to create paper money; he even forbade the general circulation of banknotes, whose emission in small quantities by the newly created Bank of France was not intended to provide an auxiliary money supply, and had only the narrowest economic significance.

Thus the finances of the Consulate and Empire, even at the highest level of the Chief of State, were characterized by a kind of accountant's minute scrupulosity and timorous orthodoxy. They depended on a metallic monetary system, inherited from the Directory insofar as the currency unit was concerned, and from the Monarchy for the metallic values of the unit. Guy Thuillier has recently called attention to the lasting consequences of Calonne's monetary reform of 1785, basically preserved in the law of 7 Germinal of the Year XI, which favored silver in the monetary circulation, to exchange with gold at a ratio of 15.5 to 1. But as the same author shows, the Napoleonic régime put the new system into effect very slowly. He even speaks of "monetary anarchy" in the first years of the new century. Coins from the pre-Revolutionary system of the *livre* continued to circulate in competition with those, more recently minted, of the new system of the franc. In the south (was it a sign of royalism?) coins of 6 and 24 *livres tournois* were preferred to those of 5 or 20 francs, although they were often worn or altered or mixed with counterfeits of British origin. Jean Meuvret once revealed the existence of "social circuits" superimposed on the circulation of the Old Régime according to the kind of metal one used in one's affairs, and the same phenomenon remained present in the France of Napoleon. Subsidiary coinage in copper, which was also infiltrated with counterfeits, was used to pay workers' wages, and as such gave rise to two kinds of speculation: on the one hand, employers obtained it at a discount by obtaining it in exchange for silver, and on the other hand, the local merchants raised their prices for necessities purchased with "weak" money. In any case, much